Blazing with the Fire
of the Spirit

VOLUME

Blazing
with the
Fire of the
Spirit

He will baptize you with the Holy
Spirit and with fire. Matthew 3:11

A 30-day Devotional Bible Study
for Individuals or Groups.

Dr. Larry Keefauver

Charisma®
HOUSE
Books about Spirit-Led Living

BLAZING WITH THE FIRE OF THE SPIRIT by Larry Keefauver

Published by Charisma House
A part of Strang Communications Company
600 Rinehart Road
Lake Mary, FL 32746

www.charismahouse.com

Unless otherwise noted, all Scripture quotations are the Holy Bible, New Living Translation, copyright © 1996. Used by permission of Tyndale House Publishers, Inc., Wheaton, IL 60189. All rights reserved.

ISBN 0-88419-472-8

01 02 03 04 05   10 9 8 7 6 5
Printed in the United States of America

Contents

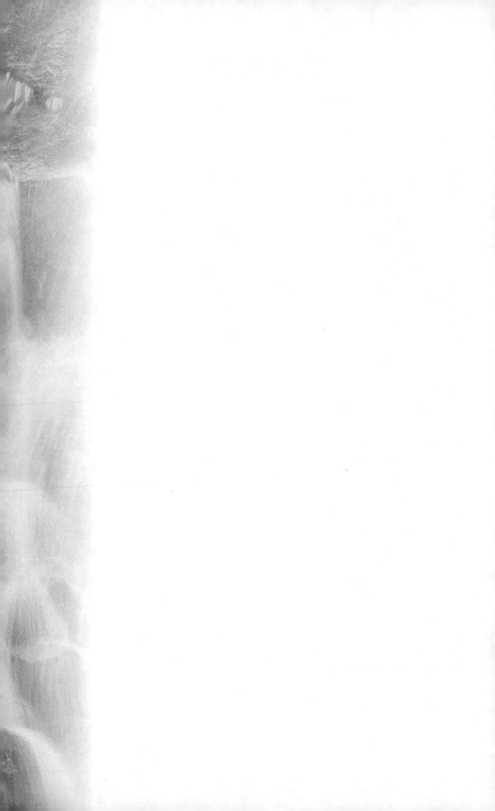

Introduction

Welcome to this devotional study on *Blazing With the Fire of the Spirit* that will assist you in welcoming the Holy Spirit into your life. This is one of eight devotional studies related to the *Holy Spirit Encounter Bible.* While it is not necessary, it is suggested that you obtain a copy of the *Holy Spirit Encounter Bible* for your personal use with this study guide. The translation used in this guide is the *New Living Translation,* which is also the translation for the *Holy Spirit Encounter Bible.*

Do not feel that you must go through this devotional series in any particular order. Choose the guides and order that best meet your spiritual needs.

This devotional study guide may be used by individuals, groups, or classes. Additional instruction has been included at the end of this guide for those desiring to use it in class or group settings.

Individuals going through this guide can use it for daily devotional reading and study. The purpose of this guide is to help the reader(s) encounter the person of the Holy Spirit through the Scriptures. Each daily devotional study is structured to:

❖ Probe deeply into the Scriptures.

❖ Examine one's own personal relationship with the Holy Spirit.

❖ Discover biblical truths about the Holy Spirit.

❖ Encounter the person of the Holy Spirit continually in one's daily walk with God.

We pray that this study guide will be an effective tool for equipping you to study God's Word and to encounter the wonderful third person of the Triune God—the Holy Spirit.

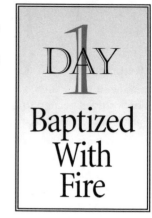

DAY 1
Baptized With Fire

I baptize with water those who turn from their sins and turn to God. But someone is coming soon who is far greater than I am—so much greater that I am not even worthy to be his slave. He will baptize you with the Holy Spirit and with fire. He is ready to separate the chaff from the grain with his winnowing fork. Then he will clean up the threshing area, storing the grain in his barn but burning the chaff with never-ending fire (Matt. 3:11–12).

The fiery baptism of the Holy Spirit consumes all chaff in our lives. The Spirit reveals and wants to burn away everything in us that is not holy. The apostle Paul writes, "Everyone's work will be put through the fire to see whether or not it keeps its value" (1 Cor. 3:13). So even our faithfulness and works will be tested for their purity by the Spirit's flames.

Chaff is a figurative type of sin that the Holy Spirit convicts us of (John 16:5–11). What sinful chaff does He need to burn away (convict you of) in your life? Check all that apply.

- ❑ Pride
- ❑ Anger
- ❑ Offense
- ❑ Lying
- ❑ Immorality
- ❑ Prayerlessness
- ❑ Rebellion
- ❑ Lust
- ❑ Hate
- ❑ Rebellion
- ❑ Gossiping
- ❑ Laziness
- ❑ Hypocrisy
- ❑ Backsliding
- ❑ Other: _____

The Holy Spirit's fire will burn away all selfishness and pride to make the interior of our lives His sanctifying crucible. We are His temple (1 Cor. 3:16; 6:19). But God declares that the heart is desperately wicked (Jer. 17:9). So the Spirit convicts and purges mankind's heart with the fire of His new birth (2 Cor. 5:17).

What wickedness has the Spirit already burned away from inside your heart? List what has been cleansed in you by His baptism of fire:

_____

_____

_____

When the Holy Spirit cleanses us with His baptism of fire, He washes away the stain of sin (Isa. 1:18). And He makes us pure and holy (1 Peter 1). Once you have been cleansed, you no longer have to feel condemned or guilty about your past. The only one who accuses you is Satan (Rev. 12), and he was defeated at the cross. So the only reason believers feel guilty after their baptism by fire is their choice to hold onto the past. And this makes room for their hearts to condemn them.

Read 1 John 3:18–24. Then summarize in one sentence what John says about our hearts after the Holy Spirit makes us His temple:

_____

_____

> *When Jesus baptizes you with Holy Spirit fire, you are cleansed, forgiven, and set free from the past!*

Praise the Lord! You are made holy, sanctified, and purified once the Spirit takes up residence in you. Since His fire is always purging and cleansing, you are always walking in the fire. So being baptized with Holy Spirit fire is a daily walk that not only cleanses us continually. We are also set ablaze with His boldness in the fire of His passion for Jesus Christ.

Ask yourself . . .

❖ Have you asked Jesus to baptize you with the Holy Spirit and fire?

❖ What is His fire cleansing from your life today?

❖ Are you holding onto past guilt that you need to let go of?

Write a prayer asking Jesus to burn away all chaff in your life through His fiery baptism:

_____

_____

_____

*S*ince we are receiving a kingdom that cannot be destroyed, let us be thankful and please God by worshiping him with holy fear and awe. For our God is a consuming fire (Heb. 12:28–29).

DAY 2

Consumed by Fire

The presence of God's Spirit is a consuming fire. Later in this devotional study we will examine in depth how God's presence in a cloud that led Israel through the wilderness became a pillar of fire at night.

The presence of the Holy Spirit comes to us as fire! His fire exposes every sin, consumes every impurity and unholy thing, and cleanses our lives.

Repentance and confession are His kindling. But the black coals of our sin need to be drenched in the oil of sin's confession so the Spirit can consume us in the purity of His flames.

We can apply the sins mentioned in Isaiah 33 to sins we may struggle with today that are in need of God's purging fire. Put an *x* on the line where you are right now:

❖ I am honest and fair.

Always   Sometimes   Rarely

❖ I refuse to cheat on taxes and in business.

Always   Sometimes   Rarely

❖ I don't listen to hate, rumor, gossip, or prejudice.

Always   Sometimes   Rarely

❖ I shut my eyes and mind to temptation.

Always   Sometimes   Rarely

If you couldn't mark *always* under each of these statements, write a prayer asking the Holy Spirit to incinerate that sin with His consuming flames.

Once consumed by His fire, self dies and vain thoughts and imaginations are taken captive.

> *When we enter the Spirit's presence with sin in our lives, His fire convicts, purges, and cleanses us so we may dwell in His presence secure in the benefits of His grace.*

Isaiah 33:16 tells us of those benefits: "These are the ones who will dwell on high. The rocks of the mountains will be their fortress of safety. Food will be supplied to them, and they will have water in abundance."

Check which ones below that you are enjoying right now:

❑ Dwelling on high

❑ Safe in a rock fortress

❑ Food provided (Jesus meets my material needs as I hunger for His Word)

❑ Abundant water (ever-flowing fountains of the Holy Spirit)

Ask yourself . . .

❖ Is there any chaff in your life that you need the Spirit's consuming fire to burn away?

❖ Are you enjoying the benefits of being cleansed in the fire?

Write a prayer thanking God for sending the consuming fire of His Spirit into your life:

_____

_____

_____

_____

_____

*B*ut there is going to come a time of testing at the judgment day to see what kind of work each builder has done. Everyone's work will be put through the fire to see whether or not it keeps its value. If the work survives the fire, that builder will receive a reward. But if the work is burned up, the builder will suffer great loss. The builders themselves will be saved, but like someone escaping through a wall of flames (1 Cor. 3:13–15).

DAY
Put Through the Fire

Fire from God's Spirit proves and tests each person's work in the kingdom of God. The Holy Spirit convinces the world of sin, of God's righteousness, and of the coming judgment for those who don't believe (John 16:9–10).

So don't wait to have the Spirit's fire test your work. Submit every thing that you do in the kingdom of God to His fire so He can burn away all that is unholy and dwell in you powerfully to use you to work in Him now.

In the graph below, shade each area of your work for the Lord at the level it needs to be refined and tested in fire.

The higher you shaded each area of your spiritual walk, the more that aspect of your life needs to have impure actions, thoughts, and motives burned away.

When you are convicted by the Holy Spirit that something is wrong in your walk, how do you usually respond? Rank from 1 (most often) to 6 (least often) your response.

_____ Repent immediately, asking for the cleansing fire

_____ Procrastinate with a response

_____ Rationalize your thoughts or behaviors

_____ Withdraw from intimacy with God

_____ Seek God's forgiveness and new direction

_____ Other:_____

> *What burns away under the judging fire of God's Spirit is anything that is of us so all that remains is completely of Him.*

Different factions were arising in the Corinthian church that were centered on individual personalities, not on God. Whatever is not completely rooted and grounded in Christ will be burned away by the Holy Spirit. Too often we pursue good ideas instead of God ideas, and only God ideas will last.

So list below three things you are currently doing in ministry to serve the Lord. Then circle whether your involvement is really a God idea or just a good idea. [Some areas may be choir, ushering, greeting, teaching, visiting, small groups.]

Ideas for ministry

1. _____	God idea	Good idea
2. _____	God idea	Good idea
3. _____	God idea	Good idea
4. _____	God idea	Good idea

The Holy Spirit wants our ministry and worship to be focused on the Lord, not on a man, building, program, or church. While good ideas may be successful for a season, all good ideas will be burned in judgment. Only God ideas birthed by His Spirit, done His way, and in His timing will survive the judging fire of the Holy Spirit.

Ask yourself . . .

❖ What ideas do you need to submit to the judging fire of God's Spirit?

❖ What good ideas has His fire burnt out of you?

> *Write a prayer asking God's Spirit to test by fire every idea you have before you implement it:*

_____

_____

*G*od the Father chose you long ago, and the Spirit has made you holy. As a result, you have obeyed Jesus Christ and are cleansed by his blood (1 Pet. 1:2).

DAY 4

Made Holy and Pure by Fire

Because God's Spirit makes us holy (sanctified and purified), there are two questions that must be asked:

1. What does God require in holiness?

2. How does He make us holy?

Holiness literally means to be "set apart" unto the Lord. That which is holy is for God's use only and belongs solely to Him.

> *When you are made holy, you're set apart as God's special, unique, and prized possession—to be tried and tested by fire.*

Look up the following passages and jot down what they reveal about holiness:

Leviticus 11:44–45 _____

Deuteronomy 14:2 _____

Psalm 22:3_____

John 17:11, 17 _____

Ephesians 1:4; 2:19; 4:24 _____

Colossians 1:22, 26 _____

1 Thessalonians 4:3–8; 5:23_____

Hebrews 10:10 _____

1 Peter 1:15–16; 2:8–9 _____

Every believer has been sanctified, or made holy, through the shed blood of Jesus Christ. This is called *positional sanctification.* Because of the cross, we are now in a position to receive the Holy Spirit's ongoing work of sanctification in which He is making us holy—body, soul, and spirit—for the rest of our lives.

So how does He make us holy? One way is through trials. That's right, the Holy Spirit uses trials to test and refine our faith the way fire refines and purifies pure gold (1 Pet. 1:7). But too often we misinterpret the trials of life and allow Satan to get a foothold. Satan comes to tempt; God comes to test.

Describe a trial you have gone through and how it has refined your faith. Write about your trial on the lines below.

My trial was:_____

_____

_____

_____.

Again, the Spirit never tries you to tempt you—only Satan does that. When you are in God's will the Holy Spirit's trials will make you strong, pure, and holy. So when fiery trials come, give thanks for the Refiner's fire in you.

Ask yourself . . .

❖ What trials are you presently experiencing?

❖ How are these trials making your faith pure and strong?

Write a prayer asking God's Spirit for the strength to endure fiery trails:

_____

_____

_____

_____

_____

*O*n the day of Pentecost, seven weeks after Jesus' resurrection, the believers were meeting together in one place. Suddenly, there was a sound from heaven like the roaring of a mighty windstorm in the skies above them, and it filled the house where they were meeting. Then, what looked like flames or tongues of fire appeared and settled on each of them. And everyone present was filled with the Holy Spirit and began speaking in other languages [or in other tongues], as the Holy Spirit gave them this ability (Acts 2:1–4).

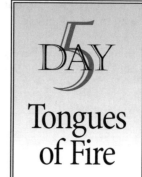

DAY 5

Tongues of Fire

On the day of Pentecost, the Holy Spirit filled Christ's followers, settling upon them with tongues of fire. The tongues of fire indicated how individuals would be filled from then on to be indwelt and empowered. In the Old Testament, faithful people were anointed by the Holy Spirit for a special time and purpose, but they weren't indwelt eternally by the Holy Spirit.

New Testament believers trusting in Jesus Christ as Lord and Savior are given the gift of the Holy Spirit (Acts 2:38) who indwells the believer forever. In a representative type of our new and better covenant, fire consumed the Old Testament offering, making it acceptable and holy to the Lord (Exod. 29:4).

But the New Testament offering has already been made. Jesus was the perfect Lamb slain on the cross for our sins (Heb 9:13–15).

> *When we place our faith in Christ, the Holy Spirit's fire cleanses the crucible of our hearts to make it the holy of holies within us in which the Spirit dwells.*

No longer needing an earthly tabernacle or priest, we are the tabernacle, and Christ is our high priest. Notice that the tongues of fire cleansed the vessels before the Holy Spirit indwelt those in prayer. Then after the filling of the Holy Spirit, the believers spoke in unknown languages, or tongues.

Complete these sentences:

My first encounter with Holy Spirit fire was_____

_____.

When I received the gift of the Holy Spirit, _____

_____.

When I was filled with the Holy Spirit,_____

_____.

The baptism of fire from the Holy Spirit was accompanied by tongues in the Book of Acts in chapters 10 and 19. Describe the time when you experienced the Holy Spirit's fire and tongues. Or, describe how you would respond if the Holy Spirit settled upon you like when He inflamed the believers on the day of Pentecost:

_____

_____

_____

Ask yourself . . .

❖ Have you ever encountered Holy Spirit's fire like the early believers at Pentecost?

❖ How would you respond if the Holy Spirit spoke to you through tongues?

Write a prayer asking for the flame of God's Spirit and His gift of tongues:

_____

_____

_____

_____

_____

*T*he cloud of the Lord rested on the Tabernacle during the day, and at night there was fire in the cloud so all the people of Israel could see it. This continued throughout all their journeys (Exod. 40:38).

DAY 6

Led by Fire

You are the tabernacle of the Holy Spirit. Upon and within you rests and dwells the cloud of God's presence—the Holy Spirit. As you allow His purging fire to cleanse you, you are led day and night by the Holy Spirit in your journey through life. His fire lights your way.

So how does His presence lead you? "When the Spirit of truth comes, he will guide you into all truth" (John 16:13). Listed below are some of the ways the fiery cloud of God's Spirit guides you through the wildernesses of life. Check all His guiding ways that you have encountered:

❑ Through Scripture

❑ Through prayer

❑ Through prophecy

❑ Through tongues and the interpretation of tongues

❑ Through a word of knowledge

❑ Through His word of wisdom

❑ Through the Spirit-led counsel of other Christians

❑ Through Spirit-filled witnesses confirming what the Holy Spirit has

　　spoken to your heart

❑ Through a sermon, lesson, Christian book, or Bible study

❑ Other: _____

You may experience the fire of His leading through a warmth, or fire, in your bones (Jer. 20:9).

> *Wherever God's Spirit chooses to lead you, your journey, even when in the wilderness, will be planned for your good, not your demise.*

Read Jeremiah 29:11–14, then paraphrase this promise from God in your own words:

_____

_____

_____

Where is the Lord leading you right now? In what direction is His cloud of fire headed? Write down where the Spirit has you now; what He promises for your future here on earth; and where you are headed for eternity.

Where I am right now _____

God's promise for my future_____

Where I will spend eternity _____

Ask yourself . . .

❖ In what area of your life do you need guidance from the Spirit's cloud of fire?

❖ How is the Spirit implementing God's plan for your life?

Write a prayer asking the Holy Spirit to guide you in your journey of life:

_____

_____

_____

_____

_____

O *ne day Moses was tending the flock of his father-in-law, Jethro, the priest of Midian, and he went deep into the wilderness near Sinai, the mountain of God. Suddenly, the angel of the LORD appeared to him as a blazing fire in a bush. Moses was amazed because the bush was engulfed in flames, but it didn't burn up. "Amazing!" Moses said to himself. "Why isn't that bush burning up? I must go over to see this." When the LORD saw that he had caught Moses' attention, God called to him from the bush, "Moses! Moses!" "Here I am!" Moses replied. "Do not come any closer—" God told him. "Take off your sandals, for you are standing on holy ground" (Exod. 3:1–5).*

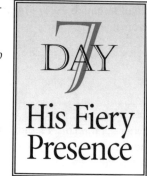

DAY 7

His Fiery Presence

God's Spirit often manifests Himself through His fiery presence. He manifested Himself in a burning bush to accomplish a number of things in Moses' life. And the same kinds of things can happen when we encounter the Spirit. How? His fiery presence serves to:

❖ Get our attention.

❖ Cause us to listen.

❖ Inspire us with awe and wonder.

❖ Humble us.

❖ Bring us closer to God.

❖ Make us aware that His holiness is near.

Now look over the above list and circle all the ways the Spirit has worked in your life when you've been in His holy presence.

Moses had been running from God. Years before he fled from Egypt after murdering an Egyptian. The wilderness had become his hiding place and refuge. But God desired to use him. So to get his attention, God's fiery presence manifested Himself in a burning bush—a bush that was not consumed.

Think of a time in your life when you were in a wilderness running from God. Describe how God's fiery presence got your attention and spoke to you:

_____

_____

_____

> *Whenever God's Spirit appears through His fiery presence, the place and moment are holy.*

The place of God's fiery presence is a place and time set just for God. He desires to draw us apart to spend time with us in communion. Jesus withdrew often to pray. Elijah sought God on a mountain, away from the crowds. Paul spent years in the wilderness with the Lord after his conversion. God's Spirit also seeks our attention. He wants us on holy ground.

How do you get away to spend time in the presence of His Spirit? Jot down the ways and times you regularly get away with God:

In the mornings, I _____.

Each day, I _____.

In the evenings, I _____.

Weekly, I _____.

My favorite time to commune with God is _____

_____.

My favorite place of communion in His holy presence is _____ .

_____.

Ask yourself . . .

❖ Where do you encounter God's burning bushes in your life?

❖ When do you withdraw to spend time with the Spirit?

> *Write a prayer asking the Holy Spirit to get your attention to spend holy time with God:*

_____

_____

_____

_____

*I*mmediately the fire of the Lord flashed down from heaven and burned up the young bull, the wood, the stones, and the dust. It even licked up all the water in the ditch! And when the people saw it, they fell on their faces and cried out, "The Lord is God! The Lord is God!" (1 Kings 18:38–39).

DAY 8

Fire From Heaven

Some days you just need a sign from heaven. Nothing else will do. And Elijah was having that kind of day. The false prophets of Baal had built an altar asking Baal to consume their sacrifice with fire. But nothing happened.

Then came Elijah's turn. All he needed was fire to fall from heaven . . . God to answer . . . God's consuming fire to issue forth from His Spirit and burn up his sacrifice. If you had been Elijah, how would you have felt? Circle all that apply to you.

✦ I would have been worrying about my reputation.

✦ I would have feared the king and pagan priests.

✦ I would have doubted that God would answer.

✦ I would have been anxious about my safety.

✦ Other:_____

So Elijah prayed and God's fire fell from heaven. The believers at Pentecost prayed and God's fire fell from heaven. Moses prayed and God's fire fell from heaven. In every situation God's all-consuming fire of the Holy Spirit manifested His power and presence. But He does it in different ways.

When the Spirit's fire fell from heaven upon Israel's enemies in the wilderness, they were destroyed. When fire fell from heaven upon Saul, he was converted by Jesus and became Paul. When fire fell on the early believers as they were praying at Pentecost, they were filled with the Holy Spirit and spoke in unknown languages. When fire fell from heaven on England and America during the great awakenings, revival broke out and thousands were saved.

The Holy Spirit gave Elijah the boldness to call for the Spirit's fire. So compare yourself to Elijah. Put an *x* on the line that best describes now where you are.

_____

Bold as Elijah   Scared to witness

_____

Worried about my reputation   Not afraid of the opinions of others

| Not willing to take risks | Will risk anything to see God manifest His presence |

The Spirit's fire from heaven burns up pride, exposes all religious pretense, and consumes every idol and enemy of God.

How desperate are you to encounter God's holy fire from heaven?

Ask yourself . . .

❖ Are you willing to risk everything for God's Spirit so He will manifest Himself in His fire and holy power?

Write a prayer asking the Holy Spirit to send fire from heaven upon you and upon your church:

_____

_____

_____

_____

_____

*N*ever be lazy in your work, but serve the Lord enthusiastically (Rom. 12:11).

Aglow With the Spirit's Gift

The key operative word in this text is *enthusiastically*. It is actually two words in the Greek—*pneumati*, "in the Spirit," and *zeontes*, "zealous." Now zealous literally means "to be aglow, passionate for, or even on fire." So Paul is encouraging believers to be aglow, or on fire with the Holy Spirit. And this is so necessary. Because whatever ministry we do, we are to do it unto the Lord (Rom. 14:7–8).

The Lord fills us with the Spirit's fire and zeal so when we are ministering to others or worshiping Him, we will be ignited with His zeal.

Jesus urges us to not be *lukewarm*, but rather *burning* with His passion, because He is our first love (Rev. 3:15–16; 2:4–5). Circle all the following listed ways you're aglow in the Spirit and on fire for Christ:

Worship	Prayer	Service
Giving	Love	Ministering
Praise	Study of the Word	Witnessing

Other: _____

Those around you will notice when you minister the Spirit's gifts with His zeal and fire. Even the unsaved will notice. Having a winsome witness for Christ is one way the fire of the Spirit burns in you.

What happens when Christ's followers burn brightly in the Spirit? List three things that happen to you and three things that happen to others:

When I glow with the Spirit, three things that happen to me are:

1. _____

2. _____

3. _____

When I'm zealously on fire in the Spirit, three things that happen to others are:

1. _____

2. _____

3. _____

> *The Holy Spirit wants to turn the heat up in*
> *your ministering of His gift(s).*

The Holy Spirit wants to fire you up with His enthusiasm for life. For example, if you've been witnessing on one level, He wants to take you to the next witnessing level. You may have shared the gospel with everyone at work that you know, and that's good. But now He wants to ignite you to take the gospel to neighbors you don't know. And to step out in bold faith the next time He prompts you to offer ministry to that stranger in the grocery store.

Ask yourself . . .

❖ In what spiritual gift is the Holy Spirit turning up your heat and intensity?

❖ How can you show others your fiery love for Jesus?

Write a prayer asking the Holy Spirit to increase the heat of His enthusiasm in your life and take you to the next level of ministering your spiritual gift(s):

_____

_____

_____

_____

_____

*A*s the sun went down and it became dark, Abram saw a smoking firepot and a flaming torch pass between the halves of the carcasses. So the Lord made a covenant with Abram that day (Gen. 15:17–18).

DAY 10

A Covenant in Fire

The Lord seals His covenant relationship with us by the fire of His Holy Spirit. The New Covenant was sealed by His Spirit's tongues of fire (Eph. 1:13; Acts 2:2).

To have relationship with us, God purges and cleanses us with the Holy Spirit's fire. So fire and covenant are inseparable. He consumes our inner selves with the fiery presence of His Spirit to acknowledge His acceptance of our living sacrifice (Acts 2:38; Rom. 12:1–2). So there can be no relationship without the fire of His Spirit.

But before the fire and the covenant must come faith. Without faith, there is no sacrifice to offer. Without faith, there is no altar built that His fire can consume. Without faith, no substance exists and there is no covenant that His fire can ignite (Heb. 11:1). So the absence of faith is like trying to build a fire without anything to burn.

Put an *x* on each line that represents where you are right now.

I trust the Lord	I'm not sure

My faith has substance for the Spirit's fire	The substance is lacking

I want an on-fire covenant with God's Spirit	I fear being perceived as a fanatic

Abram's faith opened his life to a covenant with God that was sealed by covenant fire. Then the time came when Abraham's covenant was tested. He was asked to put his beloved son Isaac on the altar. So his covenant was tested with fire after it was sealed.

God's covenant consumes everything with fire. Even our closest relationships and pastimes that could take our commitment from God will be put on the altar.

Did Abraham love Isaac more than God? Was he willing to submit his son to the fire? God sought to know this by fire. So our covenant with God—our faith in God—will also be tested by fire, because Romans 4 says Abraham is the father of our faith.

Is there anything or anyone that comes between you and your covenant with God through Christ? Circle any below that need to be put on God's altar of fire:

My ego	My reputation	My work
My relationships	My wealth	My power

Other: _____

> *God's covenant is given by grace and received by faith. In covenant with Him, we will be tested on the altar of fire to be melted in our love for Him and consumed with the desire for His abiding Spirit.*

Ask yourself . . .

❖ Are you trusting God to consume with His Spirit's fire all that you surrender to Him?

❖ Has anything been keeping you from covenant with Him? If so, what?

Write a prayer thanking the Holy Spirit for sealing Jesus' covenant with you:

_____

_____

_____

_____

_____

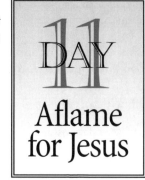

*Y*ou are the light of the world—like a city on a mountain, glowing in the night for all to see. Don't hide your light under a basket! Instead, put it on a stand and let it shine for all. In the same way, let your good deeds shine out for all to see, so that everyone will praise your heavenly Father (Matt. 5:14–16).

DAY 11
Aflame for Jesus

When the Holy Spirit sets us ablaze for Christ, we bring His fire into a world blanketed in the darkness of hatred and rebellion. Our fiery love for Christ can never be hidden. It consumes our selfish pursuits and burns brightly for all to see.

How is our light to shine for Christ? Read the following scriptures, then write down all the ways our light should shine for Christ. [John 1:1–9; 8:12; 12:35–36; Acts 13:47–48; Rom. 13:12; Eph. 1:18; 5:8–14; 1 John 1:7; 2:10]

_____

_____

_____

_____

Jesus is the source of all light. He lights and sends the fire of His Spirit to burn brightly in our lives.

What then can block the light from shining out of us? The answer is simple. Anything that produces darkness clouds the light of our witness in the world. Romans 13:12–14 describes what happens in darkness. Read this scripture, then shade in each area of your life to the degree that darkness controls it:

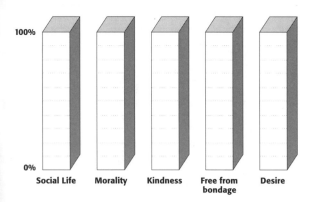

Where do you blaze most brightly with the fire of His Spirit, and where is your light burning low? Put an *x* on each line below to indicate where you are.

At work

| Blaze brightly | Burning low |

At home

| Blaze brightly | Burning low |

At play

| Blaze brightly | Burning low |

At church

| Blaze brightly | Burning low |

Other:

_____

| Blaze brightly | Burning low |

The fire of God's Spirit doesn't burn within you for your glory or satisfaction. It shines through you so others can see the glory of God and give Him shining praise.

Ask yourself . . .

❖ What releases God's light to shine through your life?

❖ What inhibits His fire from shining through you?

Write a prayer asking Jesus to cleanse your life so the fire of His Spirit will shine brightly through you:

_____

_____

_____

_____

_____

*T*his is why I remind you to fan into flames the *spiritual gift God gave you when I laid my hands on you . . . With the help of the Holy Spirit who lives within us, carefully guard what has been entrusted to you (2 Tim. 1: 6, 14).*

Fan Into Flames

The glowing coals of the Spirit's fire burn hot within every believer. We have been baptized with the Spirit and fire (Luke 3:16) and have been given His fiery gifts.

Every believer has a part in ministering the Spirit's gifts. But they lie dormant as smoldering coals until we fan them into flames.

What are you doing to fan the flames and stoke the Spirit's fire? Below are some biblical ways to ignite your life in the heat of His burning glow. Check the ways you are implementing in your spiritual walk.

❑ Praying as you are directed by the Holy Spirit (Jude 20).

❑ Coming together with believers in worship (1 Cor. 14:26).

❑ Ministering to those who are in need (Matt. 25:35–36).

❑ Seeking, knocking, and asking for the Holy Spirit (Luke 11:9–13).

❑ Operating in the spiritual gift prophesied over you (1 Tim. 4:14).

❑ Ministering your gift(s) through the anointing of laying on of hands (2 Tim. 1:6).

❑ Being faithful to the Spirit and humble in His presence (James 4:5–10).

The fiery presence of the Holy Spirit burns within you to ignite His gift(s). But in order to fan the flames, you must be yielded, ready, and available for the Spirit's use. Complete these sentences:

The gift(s) within me that must be fanned into flames is(are) _____

_____.

One way I am fanning the flames is _____

_____.

One way I need to start fanning the flames is _____

_____.

What keeps me from fanning the flames is _____

_____ .

At times, the Spirit prompts us to fan our gift(s) into flames to minister to a particular person. But because we have taken or given offense and have a problem with that person, we may not want to minister to him or her. We may feel timid or fearful, and our flesh inhibits our ministry.

Name a person below that you need to minister to, but haven't. Next list the reasons why you haven't. Then confess your inaction because of offense or fear. Finally, write down when you will obey the Spirit and minister to that person:

Name_____

Reasons I haven't ministered:_____

Prayer of confession: _____

_____

I will minister when _____

_____ .

Paul encouraged Timothy to get fervent in fanning his gifts when he told him, "For God has not given us a spirit of fear and timidity but of power, love, and self-discipline" (2 Tim. 1:7). Memorize this verse.

Ask yourself . . .

❖ What fear keeps you from ministering effectively in the Holy Spirit?

❖ Who needs the ministry of His gift within you?

Write a prayer asking God's Spirit to fill you with power, love, and self-discipline so you can fan the flames of your gift:

_____

_____

_____

_____

*T*hen the Lord said to Moses, "Give Aaron and his sons the following instructions regarding the whole burnt offering. The burnt offering must be left on the altar until the next morning, and the altar fire must be kept burning all night. . . . Meanwhile, the fire on the altar must be kept burning; it must never go out" (Lev. 6:8–9, 12).

DAY 13
Perpetual Fire

Under the Old Covenant, the altar of sacrifice in the tabernacle's outer court was never to be extinguished. It was to be maintained day and night—all year round—to be ready for the sacrifices the people were commanded to bring.

But under the New Covenant, the sacrifice of animals and grain is no longer required. We have the perfect sacrifice for our sins—the Lamb of God, Jesus Christ (Heb. 10)! In receiving Jesus as Lord, self is crucified (Gal. 2:20), and we become God's living sacrifices (Rom. 12:1–2). So we continually offer ourselves! Read the scriptures mentioned above, then write down anything you need to put on the altar to crucify self.

_____

_____

As the tabernacles of the Holy Spirit (1 Cor. 6:19) and as God's living sacrifices (Rom. 12:1–2), we must continually keep His fire burning on the altar of our hearts. The Holy Spirit's fire must never go out because it continually burns away any sin and unholiness out of our lives. So how can we keep the fire burning?

Under the New Testament, there is a new and better way. Read 1 John 1:9, then write a paraphrase of what it means in your own words:

_____

_____

_____

When the night of sin and darkness tries to fall on our lives, we have the Holy Spirit's fire on the altar of our hearts to overcome all darkness and light our walk with Christ.

If you are being oppressed by the night, what do you think is the root of the darkness? Prioritize from 1 (most often) to 10 (least often) the usual causes of dark attacks on your life:

_____ Accusations from the enemy

_____ Persecution for righteousness sake

_____ Unbelief

_____ Unconfessed sin

_____ A condemning heart

_____ Hopelessness

_____ Prayerlessness

_____ Lack of Christian fellowship

_____ Lack of praise and worship

_____ Lack of reading, studying, and praying the Word

_____ Other:_____

Darkness is overcome by Jesus Christ, who sends His fire to light the New Covenant altar of our born-again hearts. The perpetual flame of the Spirit's fire lights our way through darkness to set us free from bondage by His power. He will comfort, counsel, and teach us when He forgives.

Ask yourself . . .

❖ How is the Holy Spirit helping you to blaze through the night?

❖ What needs to be confessed in your life?

Write a prayer, confessing sin, that asks Jesus to light your life with the flame of His Spirit:

_____

_____

_____

_____

*A*aron's sons Nadab and Abihu put coals of fire in their incense burners and sprinkled incense over it. In this way, they disobeyed the Lord by burning before him a different kind of fire than he had commanded. So fire blazed forth from the Lord's presence and burned them up, and they died there before the Lord (Lev. 10:1–2).

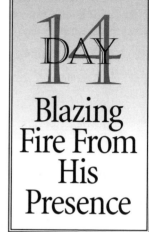

DAY 14
Blazing Fire From His Presence

Notice two truths from this text.

1) There is a wrong way to keep your spiritual fires burning.

2) And, in the presence of the Lord, there is fire.

Aaron's sons tried to maintain the fire of God in the wrong way, and their efforts ended in death. "There is a path before each person that seems right, but it ends in death" (Prov. 14:12). This may seem harsh in the light of the New Testament. But the message is this: God simply wants things done His way. And when we take the reins of our Christian life, we hinder His will while confusing others.

> *Trying to control, manipulate, or fan the flames of the Spirit's fire our way can lead to destructive consequences.*

Listed below are some of the wrong ways we can try to fan the flames of the Holy Spirit's fire in our lives. Check any of the ones you have tried in the past, then list the result you encountered:

Wrong ways to fan the flame   **Results**

❑ Legalism   _____

❑ Man's rituals or traditions   _____

❑ Trying to please God with anything but faith _____

❑ Taking glory for something God did   _____

❑ Doing "spiritual things" your way—not His   _____

We must reverently fear God and recognize the fire of His presence. We should never take His presence and the Holy Spirit lightly. Though He is our companion, comforter, counselor, and teacher, He is still almighty God. Any manipulation will be judged by Him as disobedient sin. Apparently Aaron's sons didn't take seriously enough God's commandments or the presence of His Spirit.

Read the following passages then jot down what they reveal about fearing and reverencing God:

Leviticus 19:32_____

Leviticus 25:17, 36, 43_____

Deuteronomy 4:10; 6:13, 24_____

Deuteronomy 10:12, 20; 13:4; 14:23_____

2 Chronicles 19:7_____

Proverbs 2:1–5_____

Ecclesiastes 3:14; 8:12; 12:13_____

We must seek the Spirit's fire while, at the same time, we fear it. Under our new and better covenant our fear is based in awe and worshipful reverence, not in nervous dread. But we are never to take lightly the presence of God in our midst. His fiery presence is holy, powerfully consuming all that is of sin.

Ask yourself . . .

❖ How do you express your fear and awe of God?

❖ What manipulative ways of fanning the flame do you need to stop in your life?

Write a prayer expressing your reverence and awe for God:

_____

_____

_____

_____

_____

*T*he Tabernacle was set up, and on that day the cloud covered it. Then from evening until morning the cloud over the Tabernacle appeared to be a pillar of fire (Num. 9:15).

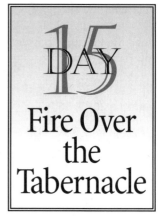

Fire Over the Tabernacle

The moment the tabernacle—the Hebrew's place of worship and sacrifice—was established, the cloud of God's Spirit covered it. The moment we are saved (Acts 2:38), the gift of the Holy Spirit establishes His tabernacle in us (1 Cor. 3:16). We are indwelt and covered by the Spirit of God, and His covering is like a pillar of fire.

The purpose of God's pillar of fire in the Old Testament was to lead and guide His people, and He does the same for us today. His fire leads and guides us (John 16:13). But He does much more. Today, God's fiery Spirit establishes us as His tabernacle of worship in which He desires our sacrifice of praise (Heb. 13:15).

When the fiery Spirit fills us with passionate love, worship, and praise for Jesus, we worship Him in Spirit and truth (John 4:24). Name at least ten reasons you have recently been on fire with flaming praise for Christ:

1. _____   6. _____
2. _____   7. _____
3. _____   8. _____
4. _____   9. _____
5. _____   10. _____

> *Spirit-inflamed worship and praise begins with passionate love for Jesus (Rev. 2:4–5; 5:13) and culminates with being engulfed in the fiery cloud of His presence.*

Read the following scriptures that describe worship and praise, then jot down the areas where your praise can be more inspired by the Holy Spirit.

Psalm 150 _____

Psalm 149 _____

Revelation 4:8–11 _____

Revelation 5:11–14 _____

Revelation 7:11–17 _____

John 4:23–24 _____

What words best describe your Spirit-filled worship of the Lord? Circle all the following that apply.

Joy (2 Sam. 6:21)   Dancing (Ps. 150:4)

New songs (Ps. 149:1)   Singing (Ps. 147:7)

Praying in the Spirit (Jude 20)   Praise (Ps. 147:1)

Glorifying God (Ps. 44:8)   Clapping (Ps. 47:1)

Shouting (Ps. 59:16–17)   Playing an instrument (Ps. 150)

Laughter (Job 8:21; 22:19–20; Ps. 52:6–9; 126:2; Luke 6:21)

Falling before Him in worship (Exod. 34:8; 2 Chron. 7:3; 5:13–14; Rev. 5:14; 11:16)

Ask yourself . . .

❖ How is your praise and worship filled with the Holy Spirit's fiery presence?

❖ When do you encounter the Holy Spirit's pillar of fire in your walk with Him?

Write a prayer asking the pillar of fire from God's Spirit to inflame His tabernacle within you:

_____

_____

_____

_____

_____

*W*hen Solomon finished praying, fire flashed down from heaven and burned up the burnt offerings and sacrifices, and the glorious presence of the Lord filled the Temple (2 Chron. 7:1).

DAY 16

The Fire and the Glory

Without prayer there is no fire and glory. When Solomon's temple was dedicated, his prayer ushered in God's fire and glory, because prayer welcomes the Spirit's fire and invites God's glorious presence.

So the importance of prayer in relationship to the Spirit's fire can't be overemphasized. Prayer releases God's fire out of our temple and explodes our praise to God. Prayer is a powerful way of worship. And the Spirit's fire burns brightly when we pray.

Read the following passages; then jot down the importance and effects of prayer:

Matthew 18:18–20 _____

John 14:13–14 _____

Matthew 6:5–18 _____

Ephesians 6:18 _____

James 5:16 _____

Jude 20 _____

God's fire from heaven is available to us, but it won't fall on us unless we pray. Why? Prayer is intimate communion and conversation with God. And as we draw near to Him, He draws near to us as we encounter the fire of His Spirit that consumes our sacrifice of worship with His forgiving grace.

So how is your prayer life? On the praying hands write all the words that would describe your experience in prayer right now. Here are some words to prime your reflections: joyful, ongoing, intimate, powerful, dull, boring, drudgery, hopeful, filled with faith, uplifting, empty, rare.

Solomon's prayer released God's fire from heaven. When we pray as Christians the Spirit fans the flames of God's fire similarly in our Christian walk. And God's glory always accompanies His fire. Complete these sentences:

I pray when _____

_____.

At times prayer is difficult because _____

_____.

The times I experience God's fiery presence and glory when I pray are _____

_____.

What my prayer life needs most is _____

_____.

> *When we passionately pray out of love for God (2 Chron. 5:13–14; Matt. 22:37), the fiery cloud of His glory falls upon us lifting us in the praise of Christ for His wondrous salvation.*

Ask yourself . . .

❖ Is my prayer life resulting in a release of God's fire and glory?

❖ What limits my prayers?

Write a prayer seeking God's Spirit to deepen your prayer life and bring His fire and glory into your life:

_____

_____

_____

*T*he Lord is king! Let the earth rejoice! Let the farthest islands be glad. Clouds and darkness surround him. Righteousness and justice are the foundation of his throne. Fire goes forth before him and burns up all his foes (Ps. 97:1–3).

God's fiery Spirit will judge and defeat His every foe. Jesus promised that the Holy Spirit would convince the world of sin, God's righteousness, and the coming judgment. So the coming of God's Spirit also brings the fire of His judgment (John 16:5–11; Luke 3:16–17).

DAY 17
The Conquering Fire

But we must understand that the conquering fire belongs to the Spirit, not to us. We are not to judge, accuse, or ever take offense against anyone. Because God takes cares of our enemies, we are to simply love and forgive them. Read the following scriptures that teach how we should respond to our enemies and write down what you learn.

God's Word	Response to Enemies
Matthew 5:43–48	
Matthew 5:21–26	
Romans 12:19–21	
1 Thessalonians 5:15	

The fire of God's Spirit goes before you defeating His enemies. You may be in a battle, but the outcome is already certain: both the battle and the victory belong to the Lord (Rom. 8:37; Rev. 12:10–11; 1 Sam. 17:47). Read the following verses, then write down how the fire of God conquers His enemies: Genesis 19:1–24; Leviticus 10:1–4; Numbers 16:1–31; Psalms 50:1–3; 68:2; 97:1–3; 106:16–18; Isaiah 10:16–17; 26:11.

Don't spend time worrying or fretting about your enemies. God's Spirit will deal with them as He wills. Your focus and attention should be fixed on Christ.

Satan will seek to distract you with offenses, anger, and hate. But he won't be able to sidetrack you as long as you release your enemies into God's hands through love and forgiveness. Only the Holy Spirit can change and convict others—and you aren't the Holy Spirit.

List below the enemies and detractors in your life that you need to forgive and release to God whose fire will convict, cleanse, and change.

_____

_____

_____

> *If you allow any personal fires of vengeance, unforgiveness, or hate to rage in you, they will destroy you. Allow the conquering fire of God's love to set you free from any potential foe.*

Only by merging your fires with the living water of God's Spirit can the fiery presence of God bring victory to every battle you face.

Ask yourself . . .

❖ What unholy fires burning within you do you need the water of the Spirit to put out?

❖ When will you release the conquering fire of God through your love and forgiveness to overcome your enemies?

Write a prayer confessing any anger or other enemy and asking the Spirit to send His conquering fire before you:

_____

_____

_____

_____

_____

The winds are your messengers; flames of fire are your servants (Ps. 104:4).

DAY 18
Flaming Servants

There are two interesting ways to interpret this scripture. First, God's angels are His servants ministering His fire as God directs (Heb. 1:7). Second, all His servants are flames of fire that do His bidding.

Consider the first. God sends ministering angels to serve you with His fire—cleansing, purifying, and purging your life through the power of the Holy Spirit. Second, God's anointed fires will burn into your life for the sole purpose of imparting His fiery Spirit through you.

So God's fire is both ministering to you and through you for the benefit of others. God will send angels when His will requires. And we have already studied at length how God's Holy Spirit ministers *to* you. But now let's look at how He ministers His fiery truth *through* you.

You have probably already encountered the Holy Spirit using you as a vessel of His fire in ministry. See if you recognize any of the following, and check the ways He has ministered fire *through* you. Then circle the way He has ministered fire *to* you.

- ❑ Cleansing and purifying
- ❑ Convicting and correcting
- ❑ Imparting love and passion for Christ
- ❑ Encouraging and empowering
- ❑ Increasing hunger and thirst for God
- ❑ Other: _____

The Spirit's ministering flames enter dark places filling them with light and convincing repentance; warm cold places filling them with compassionate heat; and ignite dry places filling them with the flames of revival. Think about how He can brighten and warm such places through you.

Complete these sentences:

In my life, I need God's flames of fire to_____

_____.

In our family, we need God's flames of fire to _____
_____.

In our church, we need God's flames of fire to _____
_____.

In our city, we need God's flames of fire to _____
_____.

> *When the Holy Spirit sends the flames of fire into our lives, we aren't only ministered to, we are also empowered as fiery ministers. Our lives can become the Spirit's spark, igniting His fire in the lives of others.*

Ask yourself . . .

❖ How is the Holy Spirit ministering His flames of fire to you?

❖ How is He using you as a flame of fire to minister to others?

Write a prayer asking God to send His ministering angels with flames of fire to you, and His fiery presence through you, to your family, and to your church:

_____

_____

_____

_____

_____

*L*ove flashes like fire, the brightest kind of flame. Many waters cannot quench love; neither can rivers drown it (Song of Sol. 8:6–7).

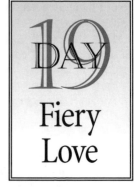

The Holy Spirit produces the fruit of God's *agape* (self sacrificing) love (Gal. 5:22). Beyond all the gifts, the Spirit's greatest work in us is love (1 Cor. 13). The love He produces in us is directed first toward Christ, then toward family and other disciples and toward our earthly enemies. The Holy Spirit's love doesn't ebb and flow; it is unconditional and unending.

> *Since the source of love is God's Spirit and its power is limitless, nothing can quench love's fire.*

Fiery love from the Spirit has the following qualities. Put an *x* on the line indicating how hot your love is (from 1 Cor. 13):

Fiery love in me is . . .

Patient		
	Quickly gives out	Is unending
Kind		
	Rarely	Always
Not proud, jealous, or boastful		
	Seldom	Usually
Not controlling		
	Rarely	Always
Not mindful of past wrongs		
	Yes	No
Rejoices in truth		
	Of course	Rarely
Unconditional		
	Always	Never
Overcomes all		
	Yes	No

The Spirit's fiery love in us refuses to be offended and cherishes opportunities to forgive. His fiery love desires the other person's best. It doesn't love things; it loves others. The burning love of God accepts other people unconditionally while confronting and correcting sin.

List three people you know who need to be loved through you with the fiery love of His Spirit:

1. _____

2. _____

3. _____

Ask yourself . . .

❖ If you have human *conditional,* or *controlling,* love in your life, what will you do about it?

❖ On whom is the Spirit directing you to pour out His fiery love?

Write a prayer asking for the Spirit's fiery love in all your relationships— first with Him, then with your church and family, then finally with your enemies:

_____

_____

_____

_____

_____

*T*he bellows blow fiercely. The refining fire
grows hotter. But it will never purify and
cleanse them because there is no purity in
them to refine (Jer. 6:29).

God's fiery Spirit desires to purify your faith.
"These trials are only to test your faith, to show
that it is strong and pure. It is being tested as fire
tests and purifies gold" (1 Pet. 1:7).

Refiner's Fire

*The Spirit's refining fire burns away
all that is impure from our faith.*

Following are some things that hinder our trust in Christ. Check any of them
that may be polluting your faith and are in need of the Refiner's fire:

❑ Unbelief   ❑ Skepticism

❑ Pride   ❑ Unwillingness to risk

❑ Undue caution   ❑ Trusting own strength

❑ Other: _____

Faith has three distinct elements—truth, decision, and action. Each element
needs to be pure for faith to operate completely grounded in truth. That truth
is in Jesus Christ (John 14:6). Below are some statements. Write a *T* by each
one you believe to be true, and an *F* by any you believe to be false:

_____ Jesus is the Christ, the Son of the Living God.

_____ Everything that Jesus said and did was truth.

_____ All the promises of God are truth.

_____ The Word of God is truth.

_____ God is truth.

_____ Theology and dogma are not necessarily correct unless they are rooted

in truth.

Here is a list of things that pollute the truth. Circle any of them you may have
embraced that are in need of the Refiner's fire:

1. Man's opinions and traditions

2. Denominational structures and creeds

3. Theological constructs not rooted in Scripture

4. Situational ethics

5. Personal feelings and/or opinions

6. Other:_____

Trusting Jesus goes beyond simply knowing that Jesus is the Son of God. So the second element of faith is decision. Faith is a committed decision to believe on Jesus as Lord and Savior. Check which of decision's pollutants need the Refiner's fire in your life:

❑ Indecision   ❑ Apathy

❑ Vacillation   ❑ Lack of commitment to Christ

❑ Lack of assurance or confidence in Christ

The final element of faith is action. One can decide to trust the truth and still not have faith. That's why Jesus commanded, "Follow me" (Mark 8:34). As Smith Wigglesworth often quipped, "Faith acts!" It requires total surrender. So until we surrender our lives to Jesus, we don't really trust in Him.

Ask yourself . . .

❖ What is the truth that I trust completely?

❖ What decision have I made about that truth?

❖ What action have I in faith grounded in the truth?

Write a prayer asking God to send His refining fire to purify your faith:

_____

_____

_____

_____

*A*nd *I can't stop! If I say I'll never mention the Lord or speak his name, his word burns in my heart like a fire. It's like a fire in my bones! I am weary of holding it in! (Jer. 20:9).*

DAY 21
Fire Burning in Our Bones

When the Holy Spirit baptizes you in fire, a powerful inner fire burns in your heart and bones that won't go away. Though your strength may fail and your body may be exhausted, your inner fire will never be extinguished. He is forever; inexhaustible.

The prophet Jeremiah was exhausted. He had been beaten and imprisoned, ridiculed and scorned. He was physically weak and emotionally burdened. But he still had the Spirit's fire and God's Word burning within him.

Paul wrote, "I pray that from his glorious, unlimited resources he will give you mighty inner strength through his Holy Spirit" (Eph. 3:16). So the fire of the Holy Spirit burning within you gives you God's mighty eternal strength.

But what can we do when we're exhausted like Jeremiah and have nothing left to fuel the fire? That's when we depend upon the Holy Spirit who wells up within us to fuel our fire with His powerful resources. Circle the following resources you need now to fuel the Spirit's mighty flames in you:

The Word of God	Prayer
Worship	Praise
Forgiveness	Fellowship with Christians
Encouragement	The presence of God
Supernatural strength	Faith

Other: _____

The Holy Spirit's fire burns with supernatural resources. Now think of the natural, limited resources you have tried to fuel His fire with that haven't worked. Check all below that apply:

❑ More work

❑ More study

❑ More classes, seminars, and conferences

❏ More frequency in attending services

❏ More _____

> *You can't make the Spirit's fire happen or grow. But you can provide the devotion on which He can pour His resources as fuel.*

So stop trying, and start trusting the Spirit.

Ask yourself . . .

❖ What fuels the fire within you?

❖ How is the Holy Spirit strengthening you?

> *Write a prayer asking for the unlimited resources of the Holy Spirit to fuel the fire in your heart and bones:*

_____

_____

_____

_____

_____

I watched as thrones were put in place and the Ancient One sat down to judge. His clothing was as white as snow, his hair like whitest wool. He sat on a fiery throne with wheels of blazing fire, and a river of fire flowed from his presence (Dan. 7:9–10).

Out of the throne of God flows His river of life, which (because of His nature) is also a river of fire (Rev. 22). The living water of God's Spirit brings His purging fire to touch us with His:

Cleansing	Boldness
Purity	Conviction
Strength	Power
Grace	Love

Circle the flow of God's Spirit in the above list that is touching your life right now.

God's river transforms sin into purity, weakness into strength, timidity into boldness, hate into love, apathy into action, and despair into hope.

What transformation from the Spirit's river of fire do you need today? Complete the following sentences:

I need the river of fire to transform _____
_____.

The river of fire needs to flow through me to _____
_____.

The most needful recent time when I needed God's river of fire was _____
_____.

As the river of fire flows through you to others, you are ignited to serve and minister many ways. Prioritize from 1 (most often) to 8 (least often) the ways the Spirit's river ignites you to minister to others:

_____ Through prayer

_____ Through feeding the hungry

_____ Through visiting the lonely, imprisoned, and sick

_____ Through ministering in a gift of the Spirit

_____ Through teaching or preaching the Word

_____ Through sharing the gospel with the lost

_____ Through giving of your finances and times

_____ Through _____

The river's flow stops when you remove yourself from His *presence*, because that's where His river flows *from*. Outside of the Holy Spirit's presence is the cold darkness. The good news is that darkness can never overcome His fire. Read the following scriptures, then write down God's promises for overcoming the darkness:

1 John 4:4 _____

Revelation 2:7_____

Revelation 2:11 _____

Revelation 2:17_____

Revelation 2:26_____

Revelation 3:12_____

Revelation 3:21 _____

Ask yourself . . .

❖ How is the river of fire flowing in your life now?

❖ When was your last victory through the fiery Spirit of God?

Write a prayer asking God to flow His river of fire into and through your life:

_____

_____

_____

_____

*H*is head and his hair were white like wool, as white as snow. And his eyes were bright like flames of fire (Rev. 1:14).

Talk about eyes that see right through us! Jesus' eyes of fire pierce all our pretenses and reveal our hearts.

If you stood face to face with Jesus looking into His eyes of fire, what would He see in . . .

Day 23
Eyes of Fire

Your spiritual life? _____

_____

Your family life? _____

Your worship time?_____

Your attitudes at work? _____

Your giving? _____

Your ministry? _____

Your sexual life? _____

> *Jesus' flaming look unveils all that is hidden in our lives.*

Jesus' piercing, fiery eyes see everything we do. And they ignite our love and passion for Him. Think of at least ten ways your love for Jesus is currently being shown and list them.

1._____

2._____

3._____

4._____

5._____

6._____

7._____

8._____

9._____

10._____

Jesus' eyes of fire are filled with:

- ❖ Compassion and conviction
- ❖ Love and understanding
- ❖ Mercy and kindness
- ❖ Righteousness and perfection
- ❖ Wisdom and knowledge
- ❖ Healing and liberty

Take a moment now to sit back and begin to pray in the power of the Holy Spirit (Rom. 8:26–27). Look upon Jesus (Heb. 12:2). Confess your sin and ask for His forgiveness. Then look into Jesus' eyes and describe what you see:

_____

_____

_____

_____

Ask yourself . . .

- ❖ When was the last time you took the time to gaze into your Savior's eyes?

- ❖ What keeps you from looking constantly into the eyes of Jesus Christ?

Write a prayer like the well-known chorus, Open my eyes, Lord, I want to see Jesus:

_____

_____

_____

_____

*W*e have the wood and the fire," said the boy [Isaac], "but where is the lamb for the sacrifice?" "God will provide a lamb, my son," Abraham answered. And they both went on together (Gen. 22:7–8).*

DAY 24
Sacrifice and Fire

God's fiery Spirit consumes everything that could come between us and God. Imagine the surprise and dread Abraham must have faced when God commanded him to sacrifice his son Isaac.

As the fulfillment of Abraham's covenant promise, Isaac represented all the joy and love his elderly parents could pour into him. Their promised son symbolized their hope and faith in God. From Isaac would come every future generation of the people of God. From Isaac would come the Messiah.

What was burnt in the fire that awesome day in history when Abraham obeyed the Lord by offering his son was not Isaac, but everything in Abraham that came between him and God. And because of Abraham's obedience, one day the Son of God would be offered on the sacrifice of fire as the perfect lamb of God.

> *The fire of God's judgmental love consumed everything on Jesus' sacrificial cross that comes between ourselves and Him. Sin, greed, lust, and the desires of the flesh burn away in the fires of His love.*

Jesus is the Waymaker who put away the sin that separates us from God.

What needs to be consumed in your life by His fire? What will you offer on His altar? Describe those things that come between you and God:

_____

_____

Write a prayer offering those things up to Him through the cross of Jesus Christ:

_____

_____

Now read these verses that speak about Jesus' fiery sacrifice on the cross, and jot down what He did to remove your separation from God, and what He desires of you:

Ephesians 2:13 _____

Ephesians 2:18 _____

Ephesians 3:11–12 _____

Colossians 1:19–22 _____

1 Peter 2:24 _____

2 Corinthians 13:4 _____

1 Corinthians 1:18 _____

Galatians 3:13 _____

Galatians 6:14 _____

Romans 7:4 _____

Ask yourself . . .

❖ Have you been taking too lightly Jesus' sacrifice of fire that He offered to draw you near to God?

❖ Is there anything between you and God that needs to be sacrificed in the consuming fire of His Spirit?

Write a prayer thanking Jesus for His fiery sacrifice on the cross:

_____

_____

_____

_____

_____

A nd the Lord spoke to you from the fire. You heard his words but didn't see his form; there was only a voice (Deut. 4:12).

Hearing God's voice is one of the deepest desires of our hearts. In His presence, we encounter the fire of His Spirit. And out of His fire, we hear His voice.

We can't hear the voice of the Spirit without approaching the flames of His fire. But when we do, because fire changes anything it touches, the fire of His Spirit engulfs and changes us.

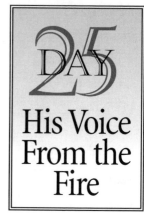

DAY 25

His Voice From the Fire

One of the changes made in us by His fire is a greater sensitivity to His voice. Complete the following sentences:

I hear the Spirit's voice when _____

_____.

I listen best to the Spirit when _____

_____.

I have the hardest time hearing His voice when _____

_____.

The Israelites wouldn't approach God's fire to hear His voice because of ignorant fear. What keeps you from coming close to hear His fiery voice? List three things that cause fear to rise in you when you think about God:

1._____

2._____

3._____

There is no fear in God's love. So read Hebrews 12:14–29 and summarize all the reasons we should approach His fiery presence joyous and confidently.

_____

_____

_____

_____

> *In order to hear God's voice clearly, we must encounter the Spirit's fire that cleanses, purifies, and sanctifies us. His fire silences every other voice in our lives, including our own, so the only voice we hear is His.*

How does the Spirit speak to you? Check all the ways you have heard His voice after encountering His fire:

❑ Through the Word (Scriptures)

❑ Through the ministry of the gift of wisdom, knowledge, or prophecy

❑ Through preaching or teaching

❑ Through His audible voice

❑ Through His Spirit speaking in your heart

When you hear His voice, the only response to have is obedience.

Ask yourself . . .

❖ What keeps you from His fire?

❖ How have you been obeying His voice?

Write a prayer asking for both the Spirit's fire and His voice:

_____

_____

_____

_____

_____

P *assion for your house burns within me . . .*
(Ps. 69:9).

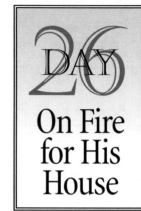

On Fire for His House

Going to the house of God can often become trite and filled with ritual. Instead of rejoicing as we approach His house, the family argues, the children fight, and our reluctance to worship increases. Does the Spirit fill you with fire for God's house?

Read the following verses, then jot down how we are to respond when attending the house of God:

Psalm 5:7 _____

Psalm 27:4 _____

Psalm 36:7–9 _____

Psalm 42:4 _____

Psalm 55:14_____

Psalm 84:4, 10_____

Psalm 92:12–13 _____

Psalm 122:1 _____

> *The fire of the Holy Spirit puts within us*
> *a fiery passion for God's house.*

Why? He longs for our praise and worship. He longs for our fellowship with one another in the unity of His Spirit. And He longs for our service and encouragement of one another.

Read Hebrews 10:25, then paraphrase it in your own words:

_____

_____

Now consider the reasons you go to the house of God. Are they fired with a passion for His presence and Spirit? Write all the feelings you have as you go to His house:

_____

_____

_____

The Holy Spirit's fire fills us with a passion for God's house. We look forward to congregating with Spirit-filled people to minister His gifts, encounter His presence, and experience the flow of His Spirit.

List five things you thank God for in reference to His house:

1. _____

2. _____

3. _____

4. _____

5. _____

A lack of fiery passion for God's house can reveal a thankless heart. Read Haggai 1:3–11, then summarize God's warning about this:

_____

_____

_____

Ask yourself . . .

❖ How intense is the fire within you for the house of God?

❖ What keeps you away from His house?

> *Write a prayer confessing anything that has kept you away from the house of God:*

_____

_____

_____

_____

_____

O *Lord, how long will you be angry with us?*
Forever? How long will your jealousy burn like a
fire? (Ps. 79:5).

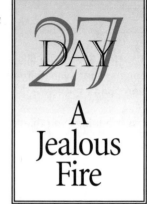

DAY 27

A Jealous Fire

God's Spirit consumes with jealous fire all that pretends to be Him. "You must never worship or bow down to them [idols]; for I, the Lord your God, am a jealous God who will not share your affection with any other god!" (Exod. 20:5).

God's Spirit demands your exclusive attention and love. He won't allow anything else to receive His honor, worship, and praise. An idol is anyone or anything with which you share God's treasured devotion. You can even become your own idol. Something you possess or someone you love can be idolized.

> *God's passionate love for us is provoked to jealous wrath*
> *whenever we worship anything or anyone other than Him.*

And God hates idolatry. What are some of the most tempting idols in your life? Check any of the following possibilities you have a difficult time resisting:

❑ Money	❑ Success
❑ The favor of others	❑ Fame
❑ Sexual immorality	❑ Power
❑ Good looks	❑ Selfish, laziness
❑ Other: _____	

Do you ever resist or stifle (1 Thess. 5:19) the outpouring of the Holy Spirit despite your understanding of His fiery passion and love for you?

If you do, what prompts you to resist Him? Check any that apply:

_____ Afraid you might look foolish

_____ Fearful of your reputation with people

_____ Uncertain of what you should do

_____ Scared of being out of control

_____ Ignorant about His passionate love for you

_____ Unable to receive His grace

_____ Still trying to earn your salvation

_____ Other:_____

Until you lose sight of everything but Jesus, you will never encounter "how wide, how long, how high, and how deep his love really is" (Eph. 3:18).

Ask yourself . . .

❖ What have you been more concerned with than loving God?

❖ When will you surrender every object of affection to simply loving Him?

Write a prayer expressing your fiery passionate love for God:

_____

_____

_____

_____

_____

*O*n each of the seven festival days, you must present offerings to the Lord by fire. . . . These are the Lord's appointed annual festivals. Celebrate them by gathering in sacred assemblies to present all the various offerings to the Lord by fire (Lev. 23:36–37).

Offerings by Fire

Fire and offerings are inseparable throughout the Old Testament. Over and over again, God commands that offerings are to be presented to Him by fire.

But under our new and better covenant, we don't burn offerings with literal fire on a literal altar. We do, however, still bring our offerings unto the Lord. And they are still accompanied by fire.

Remember Ananias and Sapphira in Acts 5:1–11? They chose to present an unacceptable offering, because the Spirit's fire didn't burn in their hearts. In fact, without His burning fire compelling them, Ananias and Sapphira actually lied to the Holy Spirit even though they had made a substantial offering unto the Lord.

What was lacking in their offering? Read the text, then describe why their offering lacked the fire it needed to please God:

_____

_____

_____

_____

Offerings without fire seek to please people, not God. But offerings by fire seek to please God and indicate the offerer has been consumed by love for God. Self has been crucified, abandoned, and set aside so the fiery offering can be set apart as holy unto the Lord.

> *An offering by fire is given in holy-exclusivity to God with no ulterior motive in us.*

When you make an offering unto the Lord, why do you give? (Check any that apply to you.)

- ❏ Out of love
- ❏ Out of joy
- ❏ Out of gratitude
- ❏ Out of duty
- ❏ Out of sacrifice
- ❏ Out of guilt
- ❏ Out of expectation of a reward in return
- ❏ Other: _____

Offerings by fire (Lev. 23) have been purified for God and made holy by His fiery Holy Spirit. He motivates our giving and inspires our motives. Offerings without fire destroy the giver and nullify their worth.

Ask yourself . . .

❖ Who or what motivates your giving?

❖ Do you submit yourself to the Spirit's fire before you give your offering to God?

Write a prayer consecrating all of your offerings to God by fire:

_____

_____

_____

_____

_____

I saw before me what seemed to be a crystal sea mixed with fire. And on it stood all the people who had been victorious over the beast. . . . And they were singing the song of Moses, the servant of God, and the song of the Lamb: "Great and marvelous are your actions Lord God Almighty. Just and true are your ways, O King of the nations" (Rev. 15:2–3).

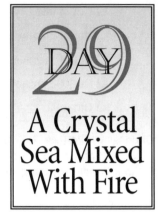

DAY 29

A Crystal Sea Mixed With Fire

We have discovered throughout this devotional study how the river of God's Spirit and the fire of His Spirit mix together. There is no river without fire and vice versa.

Now we will also see that those sustained by the pure, living water of His sea also find themselves surrounded by His fire. And that the Spirit's water and fire result in one great climax of praise at their headwaters of King Jesus.

Complete these sentences of praise for the Father, Son, and Holy Spirit:

Lord Jesus, I praise you for_____

_____.

Father, I praise you for _____

_____.

Spirit, I praise you for_____

_____.

We are always able to overcome the enemy of our soul, Revelation's infamous "Beast," when we abide in the Spirit's river of fire. Why? Because God's fire consumes Satan's every accusation and attack.

What is the enemy's greatest, recurring attack in your life?_____

_____

Now determine to praise and worship God while standing in His pure, crystal sea mixed with fire. As you stand in awe, you are not only washed by living water, you're also cleansed and empowered by the Holy Spirit's fire.

Describe a time when the Spirit's water and fire brought victory into your life:

_____

_____

> *Your greatest trials bring with them your greatest need for the fire of God to refine your faith and purify your heart.*

Without water and fire in the Spirit, you will never be refined as pure gold.

Ask yourself . . .

❖ When the enemy attacks, do you welcome the Spirit's river and fire into your life?

❖ How is the fire refining and cleansing you now?

Write a prayer asking the Holy Spirit to immerse you in His sea of living water and fire:

_____

_____

_____

_____

_____

*H*e [Jesus] will baptize you with the Holy
Spirit and with fire (Luke 3:16).

Immersed in Fire

To be baptized means to be completely
immersed. So not one part of you goes
untouched by the Holy Spirit's baptism of fire.

> *The Holy Spirit's fire consumes,
> changes, cleanses, and refines all of us.
> Our immersion in His fire sanctifies all
> who will receive His fiery flow.*

Complete the following sentences that explain what the Spirit's fire is doing in
you:

The Spirit's fire is consuming _____.

The Spirit's fire is changing _____.

The Spirit's fire is cleansing _____.

The Spirit's fire is refining_____.

The Spirit's fire is making holy_____.

Now, reflect on this entire devotional study and answer the following questions:

1. One wonderful thing I learned about blazing with the fire of the Holy Spirit is

_____

_____.

2. One way I need to be open to His fire is _____

_____.

3. When I encounter the Spirit's fire, I_____

_____.

4. The most important change brought about in me by the Spirit's fire is _____

_____

_____.

Ask yourself . . .

❖ How is the Spirit's fire flowing through you into the lives of others?

❖ What does He need to consume in you by fire so you will be a bold witness for Christ?

Write a prayer asking God's Spirit to set you ablaze with His fire:

_____

_____

_____

_____

_____

You can continue your encounters with the Holy Spirit by using the other devotional study guides listed at the end of this booklet, and by using the companion *Holy Spirit Encounter Bible.*

Leader's Guide

For Group Sessions

This devotional study is an excellent resource for group study including such settings as:

❖ Sunday school classes and other church classes
❖ Prayer groups
❖ Bible study groups
❖ Ministries involving small groups, home groups, and accountability groups
❖ Study groups for youth and adults

Before the First Session

❖ Contact everyone interested or already participating in the group about the meeting time, date, and place.
❖ Make certain that everyone has a copy of this devotional study guide.
❖ Ask group members to begin their daily encounters in this guide. While each session will not strictly adhere to a seven-day schedule, group members who faithfully do a devotional each day will be prepared to share in the group sessions. Plan out all your sessions before starting the first session.
❖ Pray for the Holy Spirit to guide, teach, and help each participant.
❖ Be certain that the place where you will meet has a chalkboard, white board, or flipchart with appropriate writing materials. It is also best to be in a setting with movable not fixed seating.

Planning the Group Sessions

1. You will have four sessions together as a group. So plan to cover at least seven days in each session. If you conduct your sessions weekly, ask your group members to complete the final two days prior to the final session.

2. In your first session, have group members find a partner to be the person with whom they share and pray during each session. Keep the same pairs throughout the group sessions. You can randomly put pairs together—men with men and women with women.

3. Begin each session with prayer.

4. Read or ask group members to read the key scriptures at the start of each daily devotional for the seven days prior to that session.

5. Prior to the group session, you, as the leader, will decide which exercises and questions you would like to cover from the seven daily devotional studies.

6. Decide which exercises and sessions will be most appropriate for your group to share as a whole and which would be more comfortable for group members to share in pairs.

7. From the seven previous days, decide which prayer(s) you wish the pairs to pray with one another.

8. Close each session with each group member sharing with the total group how he or she encountered the Holy Spirit during the previous week, and then lead the group in prayer or have group members pray aloud in a circle of prayer as you close the session.

9. In the last session, you will have nine previous days to share. Use the last day as an in-depth sharing time in pairs. Invite all the group members to share the most important thing they learned about the Holy Spirit during this study and how their relationship with the Spirit was deepened during the study. Close with prayers of praise and thanksgiving.

10. Remember as you share either in pairs or as a total group to allow each person the freedom not to share if they are not comfortable.

11. Be careful. This is not a therapy group. Group members who seek to dominate group discussions with their own problems or questions should be ministered to by the group leader or pastor one on one outside of the group session.

12. Always start and end the group session on time, and seek to keep the session no longer than ninety minutes.

Titles in the Holy Spirit Encounter Guide Series

Additional Notes

Additional Notes

Additional Notes

Additional Notes

Additional Notes

Additional Notes

Additional Notes

Additional Notes

Additional Notes